○ **Collins** gem

TH
6124
S98

Dare to Repair 2005

Plumbing

D0898511

LIBRARY
NSCC PICTOU CAMPUS
39 ACADIA AVE
STELLARTON, NS B0K 1S0 CANADA

Collins gem

Dare to Repair
Plumbing

Julie Sussman and
Stephanie Glakas-Tenet

ILLUSTRATIONS BY
Yeorgos Lampathakis

Collins

An Imprint of HarperCollins*Publishers*

DARE TO REPAIR PLUMBING

Copyright © 2005 by Julie Sussman and Stephanie Glakas-Tenet. This material was previously published in *Dare to Repair*, copyright © 2002. All rights reserved. Printed in the United States of America. No part of this book may be used or reproduced in any manner whatsoever without written permission except in the case of brief quotations embodied in critical articles and reviews.

FOR INFORMATION, ADDRESS:

HarperCollins Publishers,
10 East 53rd Street, New York, NY 10022.

HarperCollins books may be purchased for educational, business, or sales promotional use. For information, please write: Special Markets Department, HarperCollins Publishers, 10 East 53rd Street, New York, NY 10022.

FIRST EDITION

Designed by Lorie Pagnozzi

The OXO tools artwork has been provided with permission by OXO International.

ISBN-10: 0-06-083458-7
ISBN-13: 978-0-06-083458-6

05 06 07 08 09 ❖/WOR 10 9 8 7 6 5 4 3 2 1

This book makes every effort to present accurate and reliable information. It is not a substitute for professional plumbing services. If you are not completely confident in proceeding with any of the repairs outlined in this book, you should call a professional. The authors and publisher are not responsible for any damages or losses resulting from reliance on the information contained in this book.

CONTENTS

TOOLS NEEDED

Adjustable wrench

Cam tool (found in most faucet repair kits)

Allen wrench

Toilet auger
(a.k.a. closet auger)

Barbecue lighter
or long match

Cold weather
faucet cover

Bucket

Cup

C-clamp (small)

Duct tape

TOOLS NEEDED

Extension cord

Garden hose (with spray nozzle)

Extension ladder

Garden trowel or scoop

Faucet handle puller

Graphite packing string

Flashlight

Hacksaw

Flathead screwdriver

Hair dryer

Helpful friend

Metal fingernail file

Interior pipe
insulation (tube)

Needlenose pliers
(or tongs)

Lubricating
spray

New cartridge

Masking tape

New fill valve

Candy thermometer

New
flapper

TOOLS NEEDED

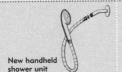

New handheld
shower unit

New toilet seat

New O-ring

New valve seat

New shower arm

New washer

New showerhead

Old toothbrush

C-clamp
(small)

Painter's tape

Pencil

Rubber gloves

Plastic sandwich
baggies

Rubber grip

Plunger

Scissors

Plumber's wrench

Scouring pad

Rag

Scouring pad (non-metallic)

TOOLS NEEDED

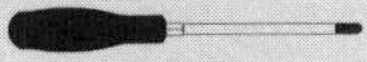

Phillips screwdriver

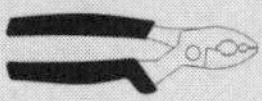

Slip-joint pliers

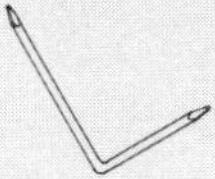

Seat wrench

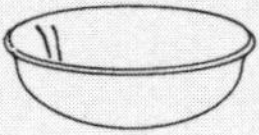

Small bowl

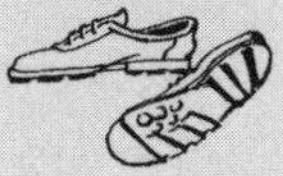

Shoes with good traction

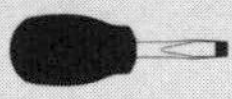

Small flattened screwdriver

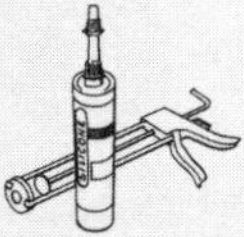

Silicone
with
caulking gun

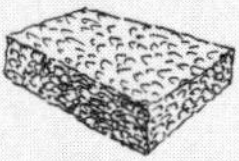

Sponge

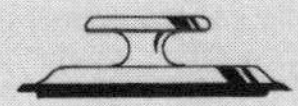

Sink stopper

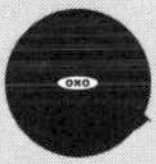

Tape measure

Teflon tape

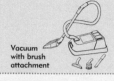

Vacuum with brush attachment

Toothpick

Valve key

Towel

Watch

Tub and tile cleaner

White vinegar

Utility knife

INTRODUCTION

W omen have stood on the floor of the Senate, rocketed into space, sat in the chairs of the New York Stock Exchange, and climbed up corporate ladders. We've broken through glass ceilings—we just never learned how to fix them!

Why? Well, we have a theory: if a woman sees a bug in her home and knows a man is within screaming distance, she'll yell for him to kill the bug. But if a woman sees a bug and there's no man around, she'll smash it, stomp it, flush it, and do a victory dance. It's the same thing with home repairs—women can do them, we're just used to writing honey-do lists, waiting for Dad to drop by, or calling the super.

We cooked up *Dare to Repair* out of sheer frustration. Things weren't getting fixed around our houses because our husbands were never home and we didn't have the money to hire contractors. We wanted to do the home repairs ourselves, but the do-it-yourself books on the market were written for tool-belted men, not for female repair rookies like us.

We knew we weren't alone in our situation: four times more women than men are heads of households. Women also make up 60 percent of all people living alone, have become the fastest-growing segment of home buyers, and are the driving force behind increased sales in hardware stores. Women want to be *do-it-herselfers*, but they haven't had the right home repair book. Their wait is over.

Dare to Repair fills the tremendous void left by other home repair books by providing basic repairs written in an easy-to-follow format with illustrations of women from all walks of life (finally, women who look like us and not the Barbies in our attics!). Each repair is introduced by an anecdote or pep talk intended to inspire you to read on.

The information, compiled from government agencies, national institutes, trade associations, manufacturers, and our own experience is accurate and up-to-date. We did every repair in *Dare to Repair* ourselves, so when we tell you it's easy, it is.

Neither of us was born with a silver screwdriver in her hand. We started doing home repairs out of financial necessity. You may have a different reason for needing to do the repairs yourself—maybe you're afraid to let a plumber into your home, or you can't take off from work to wait for one to arrive. Perhaps you need to spend your money elsewhere, or you just like a good challenge. No matter the reason, what's important is that you do whatever it takes to get started. If this means having a friend stand by to hand you tools along with moral support, do it. If you need to share the repair with a neighbor, do it. If it helps to keep a journal of your successes, do it.

If you start to panic and freeze with fear, stop, take a deep breath, and *get over yourself!* This isn't rocket science. And if this is the hardest thing you've ever done in your life, then *sister*, you haven't lived.

Think back to a time in your life when you challenged yourself, when you changed a flat tire, or asked your boss for a much deserved raise, or cared for your chicken-poxed children while your husband was overseas. Each of those victories counts as a notch in your success belt. Making repairs counts as a notch, too. Hey, it's the only time when adding notches to a belt is a good thing, so revel in it.

Our goal in writing this book is not only to teach you how to do home repairs but also to inspire you to pass your knowledge to others. When you learn a new repair, share it with someone else. Go to a neighbor and show her how to clear a clogged kitchen sink. Visit your grandmother and repair a leaking faucet. Install a new showerhead in your mom's home. Demonstrate to your sister how to use a hacksaw. Use your knowledge as a tool for improving your life as well as the lives of others.

Dare to raise the bar for what you can accomplish. *Dare* to pick up a wrench and tighten the toilet handle that's about to fall off. *Dare* to level the washing machine that's been rockin' and rollin' for months. Grab a screwdriver and *dare* to install a new compression faucet.

Plumbing problems, whether they involve sinks, toilets, or pipes, don't have to drain your wallet, energy, or time. The real difficulty often lies with getting over any fears (unfounded, of course) and motivating yourself to do the repair.

We've made this section simple so you'll want to take the plunge—we offer easy-to-follow instructions on only the most common plumbing problems. Heck, we even tell you when to throw in the towel and call a plumber.

For all you women who have never seen the inside of your toilet's tank and shudder at the thought of putting your hand into the water, relax. The tank's water is clean and the Tidy Bowl man doesn't bite.

Plumbing problems should never be fixed with a Band-Aid approach, nor should the repairs be put off, because they'll only get worse. Hell is *not* going to freeze over, *girl*, so get going and fix whatever needs fixing!

WATER SUPPLY

The Main Water Supply Valve: How to Find It and Shut It Off

As the wife of a military officer, Kathy knew that home is where the military sends you, so she was careful never to get too attached to a house. She also knew from experience that as soon as her husband boarded his ship, something in their base housing would break. Not wanting to join the ranks of a long waiting list for repairs, Kathy decided to start learning how to fix things herself. Her first order was locating the house's main water supply valve after the kitchen faucet broke off in her hand. It was rough seas at first, but now it's smooth sailing ahead.

You need to know where the main water shut-off valve is located for emergencies and repairs.

FINDING THE VALVE

Fresh water enters into your home through the main water supply line. The valve controlling the water flow through the line is typically found in the basement or utility room near the water meter, water heater, or on the front wall closest to the street. In older apartment buildings, the main water supply valve is located in the basement. However, in some new apartment buildings, main water supply valves are located on each floor in the utility room.

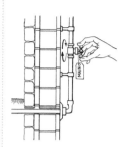

I.D. tag on main water supply valve

When you locate the main water supply valve, place an I.D. tag on it. If you want to make sure you've marked the correct valve, turn on a sink faucet and then shut *off* the main water supply valve. If the water from the sink stops, then you've found the right valve.

DETERMINING THE VALVE TYPE

The two most common main water supply valves are gate

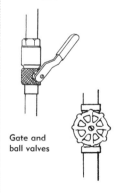

Gate and ball valves

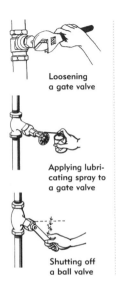

**Loosening
a gate valve**

**Applying lubri-
cating spray to
a gate valve**

**Shutting off
a ball valve**

We recommend you
test the gate valve
prior to an emergency
at least twice a year.
And if it breaks, have
it replaced with a
ball valve.

and ball. The gate valve has a
wheel-shaped knob that can
be difficult to turn if it has been
unused for a long time, or if it's
dirty. A ball valve has a lever
handle, which requires only a
quarter turn to shut it *off*. Most
new homes have the ball valve.

SHUTTING OFF
THE VALVE

If you have a gate valve, turn it
clockwise. If it's stuck, apply a
lubricating spray, and use the
adjustable wrench to turn it.
For a ball valve, move the lever
a quarter turn.

TOOLS NEEDED

• Adjustable wrench
• Lubricating spray

Restoring Hot Water to a Water Heater

> Nancy came close once to hitting the high notes like Aretha, and it wasn't because she was happy. On a morning of a big meeting at work, she was in the shower when the hot water ran out, leaving her hair full of shampoo and only one leg shaved. Nancy raced to her gym not to exercise but to finish her shower!

Sound familiar? If you're not a member of the Polar Bear Club who happens to like icy cold water, a frigid shower can be un*bear*able. Chill out, woman, the solution is easy.

DETERMINING THE CAUSE

The first thing you need to do is to find out why you're out of hot water. Possibly the shortage is due to heavy water usage during a brief time, an insufficient-size water tank, a leaking tank, or the water heater is not receiving power either because of a blown fuse or a tripped circuit breaker or its pilot light was extinguished (gas water heater).

Heavy Water Usage

If there are other people living in your home, stagger their showers. If you live alone and you've depleted the

If your furnace and water heater are located in an open area where children play, use tape, string, chalk, or paint to establish a line of demarcation around the appliances and tell the children never to cross it.

Remove any gasoline containers, paint cans, paint thinner, or any other flammable materials from around the gas water heater. Either store them in a safe place away from the water heater or dispose of them responsibly.

hot water while singing "R-E-S-P-E-C-T," you need to wait about 20 minutes for the tank to heat up the water again.

Insufficient-Size Water Heater

Check the label on the water heater for the number of gallons it holds. Estimate 10 to 15 gallons per person per day for the right size water heater.

Leaking Tank

If the water heater is leaking, replace it immediately!

Lack of Power to a Water Heater

Before you restore power to a water heater, you need to determine which kind you have.

Every water heater will have at least one big sticker on it

telling you the size of the tank and whether it's gas or electric. If for some reason you don't see any stickers, look on the water heater for a small metal label with serial numbers. The set of numbers starts with either an "E" for electric or a "G" for gas. And if you don't see the stickers or the metal label, then *sister*, we don't know what you're looking at!

RESTORING POWER TO A WATER HEATER

If It's Electric

Check to see if your electricity is working. Go to the main service panel and look for a circuit breaker that has tripped or a fuse that has blown. If the problem is not with the fuse or circuit breaker, call a certified plumber, because the trouble lies within the water heater.

> Some common reasons for a gas water heater not to work are excessive dirt, rust buildup, weak wiring, or a gust of wind that extinguished the pilot light.

If It's Gas

There are two types of gas water heaters: one with a standing pilot and one with an electronic ignition. A stand-

The gas shut-off valve is typically located on the gas line parallel to the water heater. When the valve is in line with the gas line, the pipe is open; if it's perpendicular to the gas line, it's closed.

ing pilot, which when operating correctly produces a blue flame, ignites the burner located at the base of the water heater. When a standing pilot goes out, it has to be manually lit.

An easy way to tell the difference between an electronic ignition and a standing pilot (if the flame is out) is to look for a cord. An electronic model has a cord that plugs into a 120-volt outlet or power source.

An electronic ignition is typically found in newer gas water heaters. If the burner goes out, you can't light it yourself. Before calling a certified plumber, contact the gas company to see if the gas supply was shut off.

....

The average life expectancy for a water heater, gas or electric, is 12 to 15 years. You may get some signs before it dies, such as rust around the base of the heater, greatly increased flow of water, or unusually hot water. It's important to be attentive to this appliance, because when it goes, it will dump not only all of the water inside the tank but also any water coming into it from the main water supply.

....

SAFETY RULES BEFORE LIGHTING THE GAS WATER HEATER

First, sniff the area for gas. Natural gas is colorless and odorless, but the gas company adds a strong odor to it so you can detect a gas leak. If you smell gas, close the gas shut-off valve to the water heater. Do *not* turn on any lights or use your phone, because an electric spark can ignite the gas. Instead, leave your home immediately and contact the gas company from a neighbor's home or your cell phone. If you can't reach the gas company, call the fire department.

If the water heater is standing in water, don't touch it. Leave your home immediately and call the gas company.

If you don't smell gas, then proceed.

Notice that the tools we tell you to use do *not* include a wrench or pliers. Using a hand tool may cause a spark that could lead to an explosion, so use only your hands.

LIGHTING THE PILOT OF A GAS WATER HEATER

On the *top* of the control box is a large round knob called the gas control knob (a.k.a. gas cock). Turn it to the *off* position. On the *front* of the control box is a large

Gas water heater

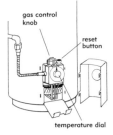

gas control knob

reset button

temperature dial

Removal of outer and inner access panels

round knob called the temperature dial. Turn it to the lowest possible setting. Now wait 10 minutes by your watch to allow any gas to escape. If you smell gas, stop and follow the safety rules above. If you don't smell gas, then continue.

Carefully remove the outer access panel. Before proceeding, read the instructions located either on or near the cover. If you don't see the instructions, contact the manufacturer.

Remove the inner access panel. Inside you'll see two metal tubes. The large tube is the pilot burner. Turn the gas control knob to the *pilot* position. Press down on the reset button (typically red), located next to the gas control knob. If your gas water heater does not have a reset button, depress the gas control knob. While holding it down, light the burner with the barbecue lighter, keeping your face turned away for protection. Continue to hold down the reset button for 1 minute after the pilot is lit. Remove the lighter. Take your finger off the reset button, allowing it to pop back up.

If the pilot remains lit, replace the inner and outer access panels. Turn the gas control knob to the *on* position. Turn the temperature dial to between 120°F and 130°F, or just above "Warm." When the burner ignites, you'll hear a whooshing sound. Turn the temperature dial back to 120°F.

If the pilot does not remain lit, repeat the process no more than twice. If it still does not light or remain lit, turn the gas control knob to the *off* position and contact the gas company or a certified plumber.

Lighting the pilot burner
without the reset button

TOOLS NEEDED

• Watch
• Barbecue lighter or long match

TOILETS

Adjusting or Replacing a Toilet Handle

If your handle is jiggling more than Jell-O, there's no need to call in the cavalry or a super. All it takes is tightening the interior nut or replacing the handle.

ADJUSTING A TOILET HANDLE

Turn *off* the water at the toilet's shut-off valve (typically located behind the toilet on the wall or floor), and flush (probably twice) to remove as much water from the tank as possible. If you live in an older home and your toilet does not have its own shut-off valve, turn *off* the main water supply shut-off valve. Remove the top of the tank and gently place it in a spot where you won't trip over it.

Turning off toilet shut-off valve

TOOLS NEEDED
- Adjustable wrench
- Flathead screwdriver

Check the tightness of the nut located behind the handle on the inside of the tank. If it's loose, tighten it by using the adjustable wrench to turn the nut counterclockwise. (Note: This is the direction opposite from that you normally use to tighten a screw or nut.) Do not overtighten the nut, because you could crack the toilet. If the nut is not loose, proceed.

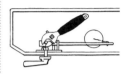

Turning handle nut with adjustable wrench

If Your Toilet Has a Lift Chain

You need to shorten the chain to tighten the handle. Simply detach the chain from the hook and move the hook farther down the chain. Be careful not to make the chain too taut—you'll need some slack.

Toilet handle with lift chain

If Your Toilet Has a Lift Wire

You need to lift the tank ball higher by bending the wire upward or else adjust the guide arm with a screwdriver so that it moves freely. Turn *on* the water shut-off valve.

If this didn't fix the problem, then you'll need to replace the handle.

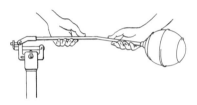

Bending lift wire

REPLACING A TOILET HANDLE

Again, remove the top of the tank, turn *off* the water at the toilet's shut-off valve, and flush (probably twice) to remove as much water from the tank as possible. If you live in an older home and your toilet does not have its own shut-off valve, turn *off* the main water supply shut-off valve.

Removing an Old Handle

Remove the lift wire or chain from the trip lever (a.k.a. lift arm). Using an adjustable wrench, loosen the handle nut by turning it clockwise. (Note: This is the direction opposite from that you normally use to loosen a screw or nut.) If the nut won't budge, then apply lubricating spray, and use the adjustable wrench again. Remove the nut and pull the handle out along with the trip lever.

Before continuing, check the length of the original trip lever against that of the new lever. If the new lever is too long, you

Removing toilet tank lid

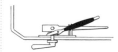

Loosening handle nut

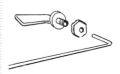

Removing handle and trip lever

TOOLS NEEDED

- Adjustable wrench
- Lubricating spray
- Hacksaw or scissors

Cutting off trip lever with hacksaw

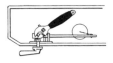

Turning handle nut with adjustable wrench

can cut off a piece of it with the hacksaw or scissors, being careful to cut where the manufacturer indicates.

Installing a New Handle

Push the new trip lever through the hole and thread the nut (flat side facing the handle). Twist it counterclockwise, but don't tighten the nut completely just yet.

Connect the lift wire or chain back onto the trip lever, making certain to leave some slack. Tighten the nut using the adjustable wrench, but don't overtighten, because you could crack the toilet. Turn *on* the water shut-off valve.

Library, Nova Scotia Community College

Replacing a Toilet Seat

> We once read in a home repair book that you should
> take your old toilet seat to the store when you want to
> buy a new one. The last thing this world needs is peo-
> ple walking up and down aisles with old toilet seats in
> their hands! There's only one place you should take your
> old toilet seat and that's to the nearest garbage can.

Whether you're purchasing a new toilet seat because
the old one cracked, you want a color change, or you've
just gotta try the puffy kind, it's important to make sure
to match the shape and size of your toilet. If necessary,
measure the distance between the two bolts for accu-
racy. We recommend you purchase toilet seats with
plastic rather than metal bolts and nuts, because they
won't rust and therefore are easier to remove.

REMOVING AN OLD SEAT

The bolts attaching the seat to the toilet are either
exposed or covered by plastic caps. If your toilet has
plastic caps, use the screwdriver to lift them up.

TOOLS NEEDED

• Flathead screwdriver • Adjustable wrench
• Lubricating spray • New toilet seat

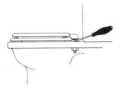

Popping off plastic caps

Adjusting bolts

While holding on to the nut (located underneath the bolt) with the adjustable wrench, turn the bolt counterclockwise with your fingers or screwdriver. Remove the bolt and nut and repeat the process on the other side. If the nuts and bolts are metal and you're having difficulty removing them, apply lubricating spray before using the adjustable wrench again.

Take the toilet seat off and throw it away. Clean the area.

ATTACHING A NEW SEAT

Place the new toilet seat on top of the toilet, positioning it so that the mounts are directly over the holes. Put a bolt through the mount and thread the nut on the bottom of the bolt.

While using the adjustable wrench to hold the nut in place, turn the bolt clockwise with your fingers or screwdriver. Use the adjustable wrench to tighten the nut. Repeat the process on the other side. If you have plastic covers, snap them shut.

Installing new toilet seat

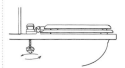

Threading nut and bolt

Unclogging a Toilet

Pat's toilet was clogged and no matter how hard she tried to fix it, nothing worked. An expensive visit from a plumber revealed the cause of the problem—dental floss. The plumber explained to her that a lot of people dispose of their floss in the toilet, not realizing that it gets stuck in the rough insides of the sewer pipes. "It's a big price to pay for 'porcelain'-white teeth," he joked. "You 'crack' me up," replied Pat dryly, as she viewed his backside in the mirror.

If you never seem to have bathroom trash, it's a good bet that someone is using the toilet as a trash can. Napkins, paper towels, feminine products (that aren't flushable), and dental floss (as Pat learned) are the most common culprits that clog a toilet.

Never try to unclog a toilet with drain cleaner, because it can damage the pipes.

TOOLS NEEDED

- Toilet plunger
- Bucket
- Toilet auger (aka closet auger)

TURNING OFF THE WATER

Turn *off* the water at the toilet's shut-off valve (typically located behind the toilet on the wall or floor). If you live in an older home and do not have a shut-off valve, turn *off* the main water supply shut-off valve.

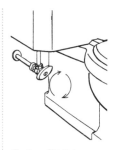

Turning off toilet shut-off valve

USING A PLUNGER

If the bowl is less than half full, use the bucket to add more water. Place the plunger in the toilet over the drain hole and rapidly pump at least a dozen times without breaking the suction.

Pour a bucket of water into the bowl to move the obstruction through the drain hole. If the water does not go down the drain hole, use the plunger again.

Plunging toilet

Inserting toilet auger

A toilet auger
can be purchased
at a plumbing
supply or hardware
store.

USING A TOILET AUGER

If the water is still not draining, place the corkscrew end of the auger into the drain hole, maneuvering the rubber tubing completely down the metal spring to avoid marring the bowl. While inserting the auger, apply pressure, turning the handle clockwise until the entire spring has been fed through and reaches the obstruction.

Slowly pull the spring back out, turning the handle clockwise. If this does not free the obstruction, use the auger again (several times). Once the toilet has been unclogged, turn *on* the water shut-off valve. If the obstruction didn't budge, call a certified plumber.

Repairing a Running Toilet

> When Retta was pregnant, she made regular nighttime visits to the bathroom. It was after one of those trips that the dam broke—not hers, the toilet's! While Retta was asleep, the toilet continually filled with water, so that by morning, water had poured through the bathroom floor into the kitchen below, across the hallway, and down the stairs. There was so much water that Retta swore she saw animals passing two by two.

Our guess is that Retta knew her toilet was running before the accident, which meant that it could have been avoided with a quick fix.

A toilet is "running" when you hear constant water activity in the toilet long after usage. Not only is a running toilet noisy but it also wastes a lot of water, and therefore should be fixed immediately.

One of the reasons a toilet runs is that the tank's water level is too high. If the water level in the tank is above the overflow tube, the water will run off into the tube, which then sends it into the bowl. (Note: If the water level in the tank is too low, the bowl will not fill enough for an adequate flush.) The tank's water should always be $1/2$ inch to 1 inch below the top of the overflow tube.

Your toilet will have one of three types of flushing mechanisms: 1) float arm; 2) float cup; or 3) metered fill valve. When the tank's cover is off, refer to the illustrations to know which kind of mechanism is in your tank.

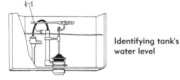

Identifying tank's water level

ADJUSTING THE TANK'S WATER LEVEL

For a Float Arm

Slightly bend the metal arm downward so that the float ball is lower than before. To lower or raise a plastic float arm, adjust the knob at the ballcock. Flush the toilet to check the level and repeat the process, if necessary.

If the toilet bowl does not have enough water for an adequate flush, slightly bend the metal arm upward and flush to check the level in the tank and bowl.

TOOL NEEDED

• Flathead screwdriver

For a Float Cup

Adjusting a float cup model requires you to squeeze the metal clip to slide it up to raise the water level, and down to lower the water level. Flush the toilet to check the level and repeat the process, if necessary.

Bending metal arm

For a Metered Fill Valve

Use a flathead screwdriver to turn the screw (located on the fill valve) clockwise to raise the water level and counterclockwise to lower it, moving the screw a half turn each time. Flush the toilet to check the water level and repeat the process if necessary.

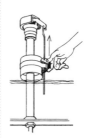
Adjusting float cup

If any of these adjustments fail, you may need to replace the toilet flapper or the entire fill valve (see following repair).

Adjusting metered fill valve

ADJUSTING OR REPLACING A TOILET FLAPPER

If the toilet is still running after adjustments to the tank's water level, and you find yourself jiggling the toilet handle, then the problem lies with the toilet flapper (also called stopper).

Turning off toilet shut-off valve

Flapper properly aligning over flush valve opening

Adjusting a Flapper

Turn *off* the water at the toilet's shut-off valve (typically located behind the toilet on the wall or floor). If you live in an older home and you do not have a shut-off valve for your toilet, turn *off* the main water supply shut-off valve. Remove the tank's lid and place it where you won't trip over it. Flush the toilet (probably twice) to remove as much of the water in the tank as possible, using the sponge to absorb any remaining water. When you flush the toilet, notice if the flapper lands directly onto the flush valve opening; if it doesn't, you'll need to realign the flapper to fix the problem.

If your tank has a lift wire instead of a lift chain, the wire may be too close to the overflow tube, causing it to impede flushing. First try bending the lift wire slightly, away from the guide arm. If unsuccessful, use the screwdriver to loosen the screw on the guide arm to adjust the lift wire. Turn *on* the water to the toilet and flush. If the flapper still doesn't work, then you'll need to replace it.

Slightly bending lift wire

TOOLS NEEDED

- Flathead screwdriver
- Sponge

Loosening screw on guide arm

Removing old flapper, lift wire, and guide arm

Attaching chain to trip lever

Be careful—the pigmentation from an old flapper may come off on your hands.

Replacing a Flapper

If the flapper is old and no longer functioning, replace it with one that comes with a lift chain and collar attached to it.

Turn *off* the water at the toilet's shut-off valve. If you live in an older home and you do not have a shut-off valve for your toilet, turn *off* the main water supply shut-off valve. Remove the tank's lid and place it where you won't trip over it. Flush the toilet (probably twice) to remove as much of the water as possible, using the sponge to absorb any remaining water.

Remove the old flapper along with its lift wire and guide arm. Slide the new flapper's collar,

TOOLS NEEDED

- Sponge
- New Flapper

with the flapper attached to it, down the overflow pipe. Attach the chain to the trip lever by hooking it into one of the holes, allowing some slack. Turn the water *on* at the shut-off valve and wait for the tank to fill before flushing. If the tank's water doesn't drain completely, make adjustments to the chain and trip lever.

After you've adjusted the tank's water level and replaced the flapper and the toilet still isn't working, it's time to install a new toilet fill valve (see following repair).

REPLACING A TOILET FILL VALVE

This repair sounds more complicated than it is, probably because you're not familiar with the wacky names of some of the parts. It can be challenging only if the nuts are extremely rusted and/or there's little space to maneuver around the toilet, so be patient. You *can* do it!

TOOLS NEEDED

- Sponge • Towel
- Lubricating spray
- Slip-joint pliers or plumber's wrench
- Adjustable wrench
- Scouring pad • New fill valve

> We feel obliged to warn you that before you begin this repair it pays to clean your toilet and its surrounding area, because you'll be very up close and personal with it, especially if the toilet is in tight quarters.

**Flushing mechanism
with fill valve**

Don't overtighten
plastic nuts,
because you can
crack the toilet.

Purchasing a New Fill Valve

If the flushing mechanism in
your tank looks different from
our illustration, you probably
have an older type, called a
ballcock. We recommend you
replace it with a newer type
called a *fill* valve.

A new fill valve will come with
these parts: shank washer,
cone washer, O-ring, coupling
nut, and angle adapter. It's
important to read the instructions, because some manufacturers will attach all the parts,
requiring you to separate
them. For example, sometimes
a cone washer comes attached
to a shank washer, and if
you've never done this repair
before, you'd assume a part is
missing.

Removing the Old Fill Valve

Turn *off* the water at the toilet's shut-off valve (typically located behind the toilet on the wall or floor). If you live in an older home and you do not have a shut-off valve for your toilet, turn *off* the main water supply shut-off valve.

Remove the tank's lid and place it where you won't trip over it. Flush the toilet (probably twice) to remove as much of the water in the tank as possible, using the sponge to absorb any remaining water.

The tank needs to be as empty as possible, because when the fill valve is removed, there will be an opening in the tank where water can pour out. If water is still coming into the tank after you've turned *off* the shut-off valve, you probably didn't close the valve completely. If all else fails, turn *off* the main water supply.

Place a towel on the floor on the same side as the toilet handle. First, you're going to remove the coupling nut and the locknut, both located on the supply tube. If the nuts are rusted, apply lubricating spray. Using the slip-joint pliers, loosen the coupling nut by turning it clockwise (opposite from the usual direction) and slide it off the tube.

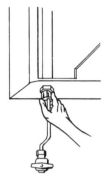

Removing coupling
nut on supply tube

You'll need both hands to remove the locknut (located on the exterior of the tank, directly below the fill valve). Secure the slip-joint pliers to the base of the fill valve, or grip it tightly with one hand. With the other hand, place the adjustable wrench on the locknut and turn it clockwise to remove. Take out the refill tube before pulling out the old fill valve.

Installing a New Fill Valve

Compare the height of the old fill valve with the new one, and make any necessary adjustments by twisting the base of the new fill valve to either extend or shorten it. Clean the area around the hole in the bottom of the tank to provide better suction for the new shank washer.

Remove the cone washer from the shank washer, if they're attached. Place the shank washer on the fill valve with the flat side up, facing the fill valve. Insert the fill valve into the toilet. While holding the fill valve with one hand, fit the new locknut on the supply tube, turning it counterclockwise with your fingers to tighten it. Use the slip-joint pliers (or your hand) to hold the fill valve as you tighten the locknut with the adjustable wrench.

Refer to the manufacturer's instructions to determine whether your supply tube requires the use of the existing nuts and washers versus new ones, and what is the exact order in which they should be installed. The most common type of supply tube, metal/copper tubing, requires the cone washer to be inserted into the new coupling nut before you screw it onto the supply tube with the slip-joint pliers.

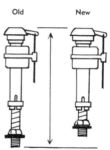

Old   New

Comparing old and new fill valves

A new fill valve is typically made of plastic. Older models are made of copper or brass.

Connect one end of the refill tube (typically black) to the fill valve. Insert the other end of

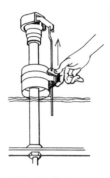

Adjusting float cup

the refill tube onto the angle adapter and clip it to the edge of the overfill tube.

Pinch the spring clip on the float cup to slide it up or down. Remember, the tank's water level should be $1/2$ inch to 1 inch below the overfill tube. Turn *on* the water to the toilet and flush. Look to see that the tank's water is at the correct level; if not, adjust the float cup. Replace the tank's lid.

SINKS AND BATHTUBS

Clearing a Clogged Kitchen Sink Drain

Twas Christmas night when Katy's kitchen sink
and garbage disposal decided that 20 pounds of
potato peel was enough and quit cold turkey! Later,
while Katy and her husband were washing the dishes
(in the bathtub), they talked of how they couldn't
afford a plumber and decided that the more "handy"
of the two would have to fix it. With the right tools
and determination, Katy tackled the job successfully.
Total cost: $4.49. Newfound confidence: Priceless.

We know that sometimes sinks (bathroom and
kitchen) will clog no matter how good you are at main-
taining them, and that's why it's important to keep
plungers handy.

TOOLS NEEDED

- Rubber gloves • Petroleum jelly
- Plunger • Sink stopper
- Small C-clamp • Rag
- Helpful friend

> Never use drain
> cleaner to unclog
> a sink, because
> it can damage
> pipes, gaskets, and
> garbage disposals.

Notice that we put an *s* on the word *plunger*. We recommend you have two plungers in your home—one for sinks, one for toilets, and never the two shall meet. Get our drift?

First remove the sink strainer and, while wearing rubber gloves, clean out any matter that may be in the drain hole. Remove the gloves.

Now here's where there's a fork in the road (*hee hee*): the method of repair you'll use depends on whether you have a single or double sink, and if you have a garbage disposal.

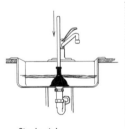

Single sink

SINGLE SINK WITHOUT A GARBAGE DISPOSAL

Place the plunger directly over the drain hole. If the water in the sink does not cover the plunger cup, add water. Pump the plunger vigorously, at least a dozen times. If the water hasn't dissipated, continue pumping at least a dozen times with each try.

Library, Nova Scotia Community College

DOUBLE SINK WITHOUT A GARBAGE DISPOSAL

Insert the sink stopper into the drain hole on the side that's *not* clogged. It's important to do this, because otherwise the water will go from one sink to the other instead of forcing the debris through the drain. Place the plunger directly over the drain hole. If the water in the sink does not cover the plunger cup, add water. Pump the plunger vigorously, at least a dozen times. If the water hasn't dissipated, continue pumping at least a dozen times with each try.

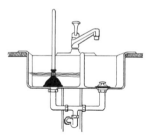

Double sink

SINGLE OR DOUBLE SINK WITH A GARBAGE DISPOSAL

For a double sink, insert the sink stopper into the drain hole of the sink that's *not* clogged.

If your sink has an air gap, you'll need to block the water that would otherwise come through it while you're plunging. Why? you ask. Because that baby can shoot water pretty far! You can block the water either by using a small C-clamp to close off the hose that connects the air gap to the garbage disposal, or by enlisting a helpful friend to hold a rag over the air gap while you use the plunger.

An air gap is a chrome-fitting dome, about 3 inches tall, that sits next to the faucet. Its purpose is to prevent back slippage of contaminated water into the dishwasher.

If you're doing this by yourself, find the hose that connects the air gap to the garbage disposal, located underneath the sink. It will be the hose that's ribbed and closest to the air gap. Attach the C-clamp to the hose to block any water from entering it.

Place the plunger directly over the drain hole. If the water in the sink does not cover the plunger cup, add water. Pump the plunger vigorously, at least a dozen times, until the water goes down the drain. Remove the C-clamp.

If the rapid plunging doesn't work, you'll have to remove the sink trap (see "Retrieving Treasures from a Sink Trap," page 46).

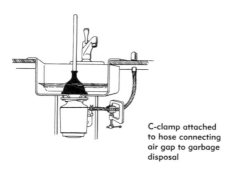

C-clamp attached to hose connecting air gap to garbage disposal

Unclogging a Bathroom Sink

> Jeryl, Rosemary, and Patti owned a full-service beauty
> salon. In the beginning, a clogged sink meant that
> business was good. But as their clientele grew, regular
> visits from the plumber caused *sheer* havoc with their
> profits. So, the barber babes took action by enrolling
> in a plumbing class. Now their money goes into their
> pockets instead of down the drain.

There are a lot of people (including the barber babes)
who would like a garbage disposal specifically designed
for a bathroom sink. But until that day comes, there are
simple ways to unclog the sink.

Before you start, notice that the sink has an overflow
hole (a kitchen sink does not) that allows excess water
to drain into it. To ensure that the water in the sink goes
down the drain and not into the overflow hole, you need
to close it off before using the plunger.

If your sink has a drain stopper, remove it. Insert the
rag into the overflow hole located in the side of the sink

TOOLS NEEDED

• Rag • Plunger

opposite the faucet (lean over and look into the sink, or feel for it with your finger).

Place the rim of the plunger directly over the drain hole. If the water in the sink does not cover the cup of the plunger, add water. Pump the plunger rapidly, at least a dozen times with each try. Repeat if necessary. Remove the rag and replace the drain stopper.

If plunging doesn't work, then remove the sink trap (see "Retrieving Treasures from a Sink Trap," page 46).

Rag inserted in overflow hole while plunging

Retrieving Treasures from a Sink Trap

> A lot of women (including us) own jewelry boxes full of pair-less earrings. Maybe it's because we think the matching ones are still in the sink drain and there's hope for a search and rescue mission. Unfortunately, the missing jewelry is forever gone to the big, bad sewer. Rats!

If a piece of jewelry, or another object, falls into the sink, immediately turn *off* the water and cover the drain hole with a sink stopper (or anything else you can find), because any water that enters the drain will force the jewelry farther into the drainpipe.

Underneath the sink you'll notice a curved pipe called a trap. The trap acts as a barrier to prevent sewer gases from leaking back into the house, as well as to keep objects that might clog the main drain from entering it. If your home is new, the trap is probably made of PVC (plastic) piping; if you have an older home and the pipes have never been replaced, the trap may be a combination of copper and chrome. Both types have two slip nuts that need to be either removed or loosened and slipped aside so that the trap can be dismantled.

You may also need to remove a sink trap if it's leaking. Take the original trap to the hardware store for a replacement if you can—be warned that if your chrome/copper sink trap is old and rusted, it may crumble when you remove it.

REMOVING AN OBJECT FROM THE TRAP

Put the bucket underneath the trap. Wrap the head of the slip-joint pliers with masking tape to prevent marring. Place the slip-joint pliers around the slip nut and turn it counterclockwise until it is loosened. Repeat for the second nut. Apply lubricating spray if the nuts are difficult to move.

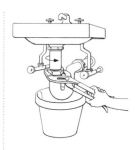

Loosening sink trap assembly

For chrome/copper piping, slide the slip nuts down and remove the washers. For PVC piping, remove the

TOOLS NEEDED

• Bucket • Masking tape • Lubricating spray
• Slip-joint pliers or plumber's wrench

Emptying contents into bucket

slip nuts and washers. Disconnect the trap, being careful not to spill the water collected in the bottom of it. Empty the contents into the bucket. If the fallen jewelry is not there, it's possible that it's stuck in the drainpipe.

Remove the sink stopper, allowing any water in the sink to go through the drainpipe into the bucket, hopefully dislodging the jewelry. If you still don't find the gem, then it entered the main drain and is gone forever.

While you're at it, check for wear and tear on the washers and trap and replace if necessary. Take the old trap and washers to the plumbing or hardware store for a matching replacement.

ATTACHING A NEW/OLD TRAP

To attach a new/old trap, first slide the slip nut, and then the washer, onto the tailpiece. Connect the straight end of the trap with the tailpiece. Slip the washer over the joint (i.e., where the two pipes meet) and move the slip nut on top of the washer. Tighten *loosely* with your hand, making sure that the slip nut is going on straight.

Place the slip nut, and then the washer, onto the trap arm. Connect the bend of the trap with the trap arm. Slip the washer over the joint and move the slip nut on top of the washer. Tighten *loosely* with your hand, making sure that the slip nut is going on straight.

Use the slip-joint pliers to tighten both slip nuts. Don't take the bucket away until you turn the water *on* to check for leaks. If there is a leak, retighten the slip nuts.

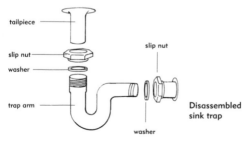

tailpiece

slip nut

slip nut

washer

trap arm

washer

Disassembled sink trap

Fixing a Bathroom Pop-Up Drain Stopper

> We have good news and bad news. The good news
> is that fixing a pop-up stopper is easy. The bad
> news is that you may have to remove everything
> that's accumulated under your sink. But you were
> dying to tackle that job anyway, weren't you?

A pop-up stopper can *stop* working if its parts wear out.
The repair is easy, but the names of the parts are
bizarre enough to be confusing, such as *clevis strap*
and *pivot rod*. But don't fret, just think of how you'll
blow your opponent out of the water the next time you
play Scrabble.

Pop-up stopper
mechanism

To fix a pop-up stopper, it's
important to first understand its
parts. Look under the sink and,
if necessary, shine a flashlight
inside. With this book on the
floor next to you, do a *search*

TOOLS NEEDED

- Lubricating spray • Slip-joint pliers
- Flashlight

and *find* for all of the parts of the pop-up mechanism. Reach under the clevis strap and push it up to get a feel for how the pop-up stopper works.

ADJUSTING A PIVOT ROD

The pivot rod is the narrow metal bar that fits into the clevis strap and is held in place by a spring clip. To adjust the pivot rod, simply pinch the spring clip and pull it off. Pull out the pivot rod and move it up or down into one of the holes in the clevis strap. Attach the spring clip to the pivot rod behind the clevis strap. If the pop-up still isn't sealing the drain hole quite right, then move the pivot rod again.

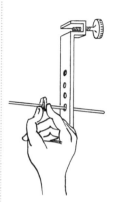

Pinching spring clip

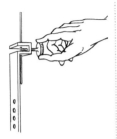

Loosening clevis screw

ADJUSTING A LIFT ROD

If the pop-up stopper still doesn't work, then adjust the lift rod. First, locate the clevis screw, which is typically hidden from view behind the clevis strand. You may need to refer to the illustrations while using the flashlight and feel around for it. If that fails, stick your head and shoulders inside the cabinet and look for it.

In some pop-up mechanisms, the clevis screw is a thumb screw, which you can easily loosen with your thumb and index finger by turning it counterclockwise. If the screw is stuck, apply the lubricating spray and use slip-joint pliers to loosen it. Push up the lift rod (attached to the clevis strap) to shorten it. Tighten the screw by turning it clockwise. Test the pop-up stopper and, if necessary, repeat the process.

Loosening a clevis screw that's not a thumb screw requires slip-joint pliers, a flashlight, and possibly lubricating spray. You may need to put your head and shoulders into the cabinet to get a good grip on the screw with the pliers. Turn the screw counterclockwise. If the screw won't budge, apply the lubricating spray before trying again.

If you're still having difficulty, pinch the spring clip, remove the pivot rod, and turn the clevis strap so that it faces you rather than the wall. Hold the clevis strap with one hand and loosen the screw with the pliers.

Once the screw is loose, push up the lift rod (attached to the clevis strap) to shorten it. Tighten the screw with the pliers by turning it clockwise. Test the pop-up stopper and, if necessary, repeat the process.

Unclogging a Bathtub Drain

When Rebecca moved in with some male friends after college, it didn't take her long to realize that not only were the guys useless in the kitchen but they didn't know their screwdrivers from their wrenches. So, she unpacked her toolbox (a graduation gift) and went to work. She fixed the knob on her bedroom door and then tightened the handle on the toilet. Her roommates really stood up and saluted when she unclogged the bathtub drain. A new pecking order was immediately established among the roosters—the chick was in charge.

Have you devised a detailed timetable for showers in your house because your bathtub is perpetually clogged from soap and hair? Throw the chart away, because this repair is quick and dirty.

TUB WITH A POP-UP STOPPER

Flip up the drain lever, which is located on the overflow plate cover. Turn the stopper counterclockwise to loosen. Pull out the stopper and remove any accumulation of

TOOLS NEEDED
• Needlenose pliers • Flathead screwdriver
• Rag • Plunger

hair. If the water recedes down the drain, then you've solved the problem. Insert the stopper into the drain.

TUB WITH A REMOVABLE STRAINER

Step into the tub and insert the needlenose pliers into two of the holes in the strainer. With a tight grip on the pliers, turn the strainer counterclockwise to remove it (you may need to use one hand on each handle of the pliers to exert more force). Once the strainer is out, remove any accumulation of hair. If the water recedes, then the problem is solved. Insert the strainer into the drain hole and turn it clockwise, making certain to get a tight seal.

Drain lever in "up" position

Removing strainer

IF THE DRAIN IS STILL CLOGGED

Use the flathead screwdriver to remove the screw(s) from the overflow plate cover. Take off the cover and stuff a rag into the hole to provide greater suction.

Place the plunger directly over the drain hole. If the water doesn't cover the plunger's cup, add water to the tub. Plunge rapidly about a dozen times. Remove the plunger, allowing the water to recede down the drain.

Stuffing rag
into overflow hole

Replacing Sealant Around a Bathtub

> Cristina and Alexandra have been neighbors for years,
> helping paint each other's houses, install dimmer
> switches, and clean gutters. So, when it was time for
> Cristina to recaulk her bathtubs, she asked her friend
> for some neighborly help. Together they removed and
> replaced the sealant around all three bathtubs, while
> sharing family stories, and when the job was done
> they shared the bill for a great lunch out.

Even if you're not having a friend help you with this
project, you still need to clean the bathtub and tile before beginning. Sealants will adhere properly to the joint
only if the area is free of mildew and dirt.

The place where the bathtub and tile meet is called
the joint. This is where water from showers and baths
can cause mildew and damage to tiles and walls, which
could mean big bucks. Therefore, it's vital to protect the
joint with a protective rubber-type sealant, such as silicone. You'll know when to replace the sealant when you
see cracks or erosion.

TOOLS NEEDED

- Painter's tape • Flathead screwdriver • Tub and tile cleaner
- Rag • Silicone with caulking gun • Scissors
- Rubber gloves

> Silicone is a permanent adhesive, which means that if it dries on your skin or clothing, it may be difficult to remove.

Silicone comes in small tubes that you can squeeze like toothpaste to apply the caulk around the tub, or in larger tubes that fit into a caulking gun. If you have more than one bathtub in your home, stagger replacing the sealant on the others, because the drying time can be as much as 24 hours or more.

REMOVING OLD SEALANT

First, attach painter's tape above and below the joint to prevent scratching the tub and tile when you're removing the sealant. Use a flathead screwdriver to pry loose the sealant from around the tub. If the sealant is a sili-

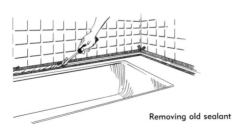

Removing old sealant

cone caulking, you'll be able to pull a lot of it out with your fingers; if it's grout, you'll need to scrape away at it with the screwdriver. Once all of the sealant has been removed, clean the area of any mildew or dirt and dry completely with a rag.

If you want to paint over the sealant, purchase a silicone whose label states it is paintable. As always, read the manufacturer's instructions before beginning.

PREPARING NEW SEALANT
For sealant in a hand-held tube, remove the sealant's cap. Use the scissors to cut off the tip of the nozzle at an angle to produce the desired size of bead. For sealant in a large tube, create a hole in the opening by using the seal puncture on the caulking gun and load the tube into the gun.

Cutting off tip of caulking tube

APPLYING NEW SEALANT

Starting at one end of the tub, apply the silicone along the joint in a thin bead. Wearing rubber gloves, use one finger to gently smooth any uneven caulking. Remove the painter's tape. Dampen a rag and wipe away any caulking that went astray on the tiles or tub.

For recaulking around the base of the tub (where it meets the flooring), follow the same steps.

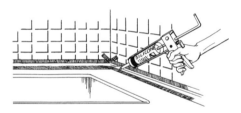

**Applying caulking
around tub**

FAUCETS

Repairing a Leaking Faucet

> The road to hell is paved with good intentions.
> So is the road to a plumber's wallet. Therefore,
> don't start this project without reading up on
> faucets first, and never tackle this project on a
> weekend or holiday when plumbers charge extra.
> Not that we don't have full confidence in you!

You know the old saying "You can't tell a book by its
cover"? Well, the same holds true for faucets. All
faucets have a spout and one or two handles, but the
differences among them are not based on looks but
on what lies inside. Therefore,
you might not know which
type you have until you disassemble it. Of course, it's best
to always take the parts to
a plumbing supply or hardware store when purchasing
replacements.

> Because there are
> so many different
> styles of faucets,
> these repairs are
> for only the most
> common types.

Faucets are divided into four categories based on their interior mechanisms: *compression*, *ball-type*, *cartridge*, and *disk*. A *compression* faucet, the oldest type, typically has two handles. Most kitchen faucets are either *ball-type* or *cartridge*. A *ball-type* faucet's handle rotates, while the handles of *cartridge* and *disk* faucets move up and down. A *disk* faucet, a combination of a ball-type and cartridge faucet, is the high end faucet type, because its disk assembly rarely has to be replaced.

Did you know that the location of the drip determines the cause, thereby determining the solution? We give repair instructions for faucets with leaks originating at the spout and for those with leaks from the handle/base.

Before doing any repair work *on* a faucet, remember to turn *off* the water at the sink's shut-off valve (located underneath the sink) or at the main shut-off valve before beginning. Turn *on* the sink and shower faucets to drain the water from the pipes on the level where you're working and the floor above, if applicable.

COMPRESSION FAUCET

If the Faucet Leaks from the Spout

When the handles are turned *off* and water drips from the spout, then the problem may lie with a damaged washer, seat, or stem.

Turn *off* the water at the sink's shut-off valve (located underneath the sink) or at the main water supply shut-off valve. Cover the sink drain to prevent small parts from entering. Move the handle to the *on* position to drain any water.

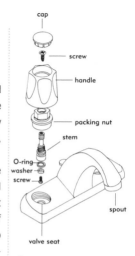

Compression faucet stem assembly

If your faucet has a cap on top, pop it off with the metal fingernail file. Use the screwdriver to remove the screw on each handle, and lift off the handles. If you are unable

TOOLS NEEDED

- Metal fingernail file • Screwdriver (Phillips or flathead)
- Faucet handle puller • Slip-joint pliers
- Plastic sandwich baggie

to remove a handle, use the faucet handle puller to extract it. Place the sidebars of the puller under the handle. Turn the bar at the top of the puller so that the shaft is inserted into the handle. Tighten the bar and pull out the handle.

Handle puller inserted into faucet stem

To remove a stem, place the slip-joint pliers around the packing nut of the stem and loosen by turning it counterclockwise. Lift out the stem with your hand or pliers, and place inside a baggie. Repeat the procedure for the other stem. Take the baggie, with the two stems intact, to a plumbing supply or hardware store to purchase new stems, washers, or valve seats.

Installing a New Washer

Using the screwdriver, remove the stem screw and pry out the old washer. Replace it with the new washer. Insert the stem screw and tighten. Repeat the procedure on the other stem.

TOOLS NEEDED
• Screwdriver (Phillips or flathead) • New washer

Installing a New Valve Seat

It's important to replace the valve seat while you're replacing a washer, because a worn valve seat will damage a new washer. To find out if the valve seat is worn, insert a finger into the faucet body (where the valve seat is located) and rub around the edge. If it feels rough, then the valve seat is deteriorated.

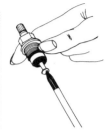

Removing stem screw

To remove the old valve seat, use the appropriate-size end of the seat wrench (L-shaped) and insert it into the faucet body. Turn it counterclockwise to loosen the valve seat. Remove it from the faucet body.

Removing valve seat

Apply several layers of Teflon tape counterclockwise onto the new valve seat. Place the new valve seat on the appropriate-size end of the seat wrench and insert it

TOOLS NEEDED

• Seat wrench • Teflon tape • New valve seat

> **Teflon tape is a white, thin, pliable tape that wraps around pipe threads to prevent pressure leaks.**

into the faucet body, avoiding an uneven threading. Turn it clockwise to tighten.

Reinserting an Original Stem or Installing a New Stem with a New O-Ring

You have the option of replacing just the O-ring instead of the stem if you want to save money. However, since you have to take out the stem to remove the O-ring, it makes sense to install a new stem as well.

Before installing the new stem (or reinstalling the original), make sure it is in a fully retracted (i.e., open) position. If you are using the original stem and it came equipped with an O-ring, carefully cut it off, using a utility knife, and place the new O-ring on it.

Place the stem in the faucet body and tighten by hand. Use the slip-joint pliers to tighten the packing nut on the stem, turning it clockwise.

Before replacing the handles, turn the water *on* at

TOOLS NEEDED
- Utility knife • New O-ring • New stem (includes a new O-ring)
- Slip-joint pliers • Graphite packing string

either the sink's shut-off valve or the main water supply shut-off valve to test for leaks. If leaks occur, it could be that the packing nut simply needs another quarter turn. Or the problem could be that the stem was not properly installed in the faucet body.

Turn *off* the water again. Tighten the packing nut, making sure that you don't overtighten, because doing so could restrict movement of the stem and make it difficult to turn the faucets on and off. If so, then remove the packing nut and apply graphite packing string on the nut and replace.

If the stem is causing the problem, remove and reinsert it, being careful to evenly thread it into the faucet body. Tighten securely without overtightening.

If a Faucet Leaks from the Handle/Base

We know this is weird, but the instructions (including tools) for this repair are the same as for "Reinserting an Original Stem or Installing a New Stem with a New O-Ring" (page 66). The reason is that the O-ring is located on the stem and the only way to replace it is to remove the stem. So, follow all of the above instructions to the very last *drop!*

BALL-TYPE FAUCET

If the Faucet Leaks from the Spout

When the handle is turned off and the faucet leaks from the spout, the problem could be a loose adjusting ring, a damaged ball, worn valve seats, or worn springs. Before replacing any parts, first try tightening the adjusting ring.

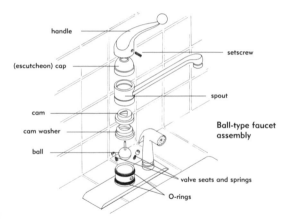

handle

setscrew

(escutcheon) cap

spout

cam

cam washer

ball

Ball-type faucet assembly

valve seats and springs

O-rings

TOOLS NEEDED

- Allen wrench set (aka folding hex key set)
- Cam tool (found in most faucet repair kits)

Tightening the Adjusting Ring or Dome Housing

Find the right-size Allen wrench to fit into the hole underneath the handle. Turn the Allen wrench counterclockwise to loosen the setscrew. Lift off the handle.

Removing setscrew

Insert the cam tool into the adjusting ring (located in the cap) and turn clockwise to tighten, making certain not to over-tighten and crack the handle.

> **Not all ball-type faucets have an adjusting ring or dome housing.**

Replace the handle and setscrew and test for leaks. If the spout still leaks, then you'll need to replace the worn parts.

Replacing a Damaged Ball, Valve Seats, and Springs

Turn *off* the water at the sink's shut-off valve (located underneath the sink), or at the main water supply shut-off valve. Cover the sink drain to prevent small parts from entering. Move the handle to the *on* position to drain any water.

Aligning notches on cam and faucet body

Find the right-size Allen wrench to fit into the hole underneath the handle. Turn the Allen wrench counterclockwise to loosen the setscrew. Lift off the handle. Tape the screw to the handle, so you won't lose it.

Tape the head of the slip-joint pliers to prevent marring. Place the pliers on the grooves of the cap, turning counterclockwise to loosen. Lift off the cap.

Pull out the cam, cam washer, and ball with your fingers (noting the position of the ball) and place in a baggie. If the ball is worn, you'll need to replace it (purchase only a metal ball, because it will last longer).

Using a screwdriver, remove the springs and valve seats from the faucet body and place in a separate baggie. Take the springs and valve seats (and the worn ball, if applicable) to a plumbing supply or hardware store and purchase replacements.

Insert the new springs and valve seats into the faucet body. Position the ball the same way you found it. Place the cam washer and cam back in the faucet, making sure that the notch on the cam fits into the slot on the faucet body. Reattach the cap and tighten with the adjustable wrench. Replace the handle and insert the screw. Tighten it with the Allen wrench. Turn the water *on* at the sink's shut-off valve or the main water supply shut-off valve.

If the Faucet Leaks from the Handle/Base

Damaged O-rings are to blame and will need to be replaced.

TOOLS NEEDED

- Allen wrench • Masking tape • Slip-joint pliers
- Plastic sandwich baggie • Screwdriver (flathead or Phillips)

Replacing the O-rings

Turn *off* the water at the sink's shut-off valve (located underneath the sink), or at the main water supply shut-off valve. Cover the sink drain to prevent small parts from entering. Move the handle to the *on* position to drain any water.

Find the right-size Allen wrench to fit into the hole underneath the handle. Turn the Allen wrench counterclockwise to loosen the setscrew. Lift off the handle.

Tape the head of the slip-joint pliers to prevent marring. Place the pliers on the grooves of the cap, turning it counterclockwise to loosen. Lift off the cap.

Pull out the cam, cam washer, ball, valve seats, and springs with your fingers (noting the position of the ball) and place in a baggie.

Remove the spout by twisting it upward. Use the utility knife to cut off the O-rings. Install the new O-rings, replace the spout, and reassemble the faucet. Turn *on* the water at the sink's or main water supply shut-off valve and test for leaks.

TOOLS NEEDED

• Allen wrench • Masking tape • Slip-joint pliers
• Plastic sandwich baggie • Utility knife • New O-rings

CARTRIDGE FAUCET

If the faucet leaks from the spout, the problem lies with the cartridge. If the leak originates at the handle/base, then worn O-rings are to blame. Typically this is where we'd tell you to replace either the worn cartridge or the O-rings, but because the O-rings are located on the cartridge, it makes sense to replace both, no matter the source of the leak.

Turn *off* the water at the sink's shut-off valve (located underneath the sink) or at the main water supply shut-off valve. Cover the sink drain to prevent small parts from entering. Move the handle to the *on* position to drain any excess water.

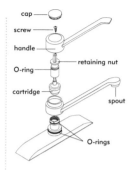

Cartridge faucet assembly

TOOLS NEEDED

- Metal fingernail file
- Screwdriver (flathead or Phillips)
- Masking tape • Slip-joint pliers
- New O-rings • New cartridge
- Plastic sandwich baggie

Removing the Old Cartridge

Pop off the cap with the metal fingernail file. Use the screw-

Removing retaining nut

driver to loosen the screw. Lift up and tilt the handle to re-move it. Pry off the retaining nut with the screwdriver or, if it's stuck, use slip-joint pliers (with the head wrapped in masking tape to prevent scratching the surface). Place the pliers on the retaining nut (ring), turning it counter-clockwise to loosen. If there is a retaining clip (U-shaped) located on the side of the stem, remove it with pliers. Tape the retaining clip to the handle for safekeeping.

Grasp the top of the cartridge with the slip-joint pliers and pull the cartridge straight up and out. Place the cartridge inside a baggie and take it to the plumbing supply or hardware store for replacement.

Removing the Original O-rings

To remove the spout, twist upward and pull it off. Using the utility knife, carefully cut the worn O-rings from the faucet body.

Installing New O-rings and Cartridge

Place the new O-rings on the grooved parts of the faucet body. Install the spout and then the cartridge. It's really important that you place the new cartridge so that its tab faces forward.

If there is a retaining clip, replace it now. Return the retainer nut and use the slip-joint pliers to tighten it by turning it clockwise. Replace the handle, screw, and cap. Turn *on* the water and check for leaks. If the hot and cold water are reversed (*oops!*), go back and turn the cartridge 180 degrees.

DISK FAUCET

A disk faucet usually leaks because of deposit buildup on the rubber seals or between the ceramic disks. If the faucet still leaks after you've cleaned the seals, you'll need to replace the entire disk assembly.

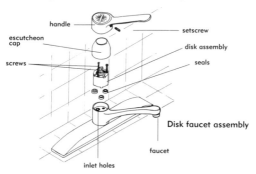

handle

setscrew

escutcheon cap

disk assembly

screws

seals

Disk faucet assembly

faucet

inlet holes

Cleaning the Seals

Turn *off* the water at the sink's shut-off valve (located underneath the sink), or at the main water supply shut-off

TOOLS NEEDED

- Allen wrench • Masking tape • Slip-joint pliers
- White vinegar • Plastic sandwich baggie
- Screwdriver (flathead or Phillips) • Scouring pad (nonmetallic)

Removing rubber seals

valve. Cover the sink drain to prevent small parts from entering. Move the handle to the *on* position to drain any excess water.

Find the right-size Allen wrench to fit the setscrew in the handle. Turn the Allen wrench counterclockwise to loosen the screw. Lift off the handle. Tape the head of the slip-joint pliers to prevent scratching the finish. Place the pliers on the escutcheon cap (dome housing), turning it counterclockwise to loosen. Remove the cap.

Use the Phillips screwdriver to remove the 3 screws located in the disk assembly, and pull the assembly out while noting its position. Carefully remove the 3 rubber seals on the bottom of the cylinder, using the flathead screwdriver. If the seals aren't worn, clean them with a nonmetallic scouring pad or toothbrush. Soak the cylinder in vinegar to eliminate deposit buildup in the inlet holes, which house the seals.

If the seals are worn, place them with the cylinder in a baggie and take them to a plumbing supply or hardware store for replacement.

Installing the Seals

Insert the original or new seals into the inlet holes. Place the disk assembly in the faucet body, aligning the holes on the bottom of the disk assembly with the holes in the faucet body. Return the 3 screws and tighten them with the Phillips screwdriver. Replace the escutcheon cap and handle, and fasten the setscrew into the handle with the Allen wrench.

After you've returned all of the faucet parts, it's extremely important to turn the handle to the *on* position **before** turning the water supply *on*, because a sudden surge of air can crack the ceramic disks. So, the best thing to do is to turn *on* the water supply *slowly*.

If the faucet still leaks, the disk assembly needs to be replaced. Take the old disk assembly to the plumbing supply or hardware store for replacement. (Note: The new disk assembly will include seals.)

Unclogging a Sink Spray

> Grace got tired of writing honey-do lists only never to see anything scratched off. So, on the first Sunday of the football season, she left her husband in front of the TV and went to the local hardware store. She returned with a game plan and equipment to fix the sink spray that hadn't worked since the Miami Dolphins had a perfect record. During the football season, she tackled a project every week. Her husband, thrilled by her new talent, called her the "Repair Fairy," because things "magically" got fixed around the house. Grace smiled and said, "That's nice, honey. Just don't think about leaving your teeth under the pillow."

A sink spray is a great kitchen gadget . . . when it works. When it doesn't, you can score a touchdown, just like Grace, by doing this easy repair.

The difference between an older model sink spray and a new one is simply in how you clean it. To clean a new sink spray, you have to disconnect it at the hose; to clean an older model, you have to dismantle the head.

TOOLS NEEDED

• Small flathead screwdriver • Plastic sandwich baggies
• White vinegar • Small bowl • Old toothbrush • Toothpick

If in doubt about which kind you own, try to disassemble the sink spray to find out.

UNCLOGGING AN OLDER MODEL

A sink spray will have either a screw that's visible, or one that's hidden behind a cover. If the screw is hidden, use the small screwdriver to pry the cover off, and remove the screw. Take out the perforated disk, sleeve, and washers and place all of these parts along with the screw in a baggie. (You may feel more comfortable putting each part in a separate baggie and labeling each baggie with a number corresponding to the part you removed first.)

Soak the cover in vinegar for at least 1 to $1\frac{1}{2}$ hours. Remove

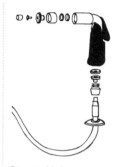

Disassembled sink spray

the cover and scrub gently with a toothbrush. Poke the holes with a toothpick and rinse with warm water. Replace the parts in the opposite order, starting with the washer.

Spray head soaking in vinegar

UNCLOGGING A NEWER MODEL

Turn the spray head counter-clockwise to unscrew it from the hose. Soak the entire spray head in a bowl of vinegar for at least 1 to $1\frac{1}{2}$ hours. Poke the holes with a toothpick. Rinse the spray head with warm water and screw it back onto the hose.

Replacing a Showerhead and Shower Arm

> While lying in your bed at night, are you counting water droplets instead of sheep? Stop the water torture and replace your broken showerhead.

Replacing a showerhead, whether because it's leaking or because you want a fancier model, is an easy project. But, just as with any plumbing repair, stuff happens—a nut may be hard to loosen, a leak suddenly appears, etc. Don't panic, because even the most seasoned plumber can encounter unexpected problems.

We recommend you remove the showerhead and take it to the hardware store before purchasing another—not because we want you to be stuck with the same style, but because a new showerhead needs to fit onto the existing shower arm. Or, you can replace the shower arm to fit the new showerhead. It's easy to do . . . really!

TOOLS NEEDED

- Masking tape • Slip-joint pliers or plumber's wrench
- Adjustable wrench • Lubricating spray • Old toothbrush
- Teflon tape • New showerhead • New shower arm
- Rubber grip

Slip-joint pliers
and adjustable
wrench on
shower arm

Teflon tape is
white, thin, pliable
tape that wraps
around pipe threads
to prevent pressure
leaks.

REPLACING A SHOWERHEAD

Removing an Old Showerhead

Before starting, wrap masking tape around the heads of the slip-joint pliers and adjustable wrench to prevent marring. Attach the pliers to the top of the shower arm to keep it from rotating. Position the adjustable wrench on the collar nut and turn it counterclockwise. If the nut is difficult to unscrew, apply a lubricating spray to it. Once the nut is loose, you can continue unscrewing it with your hand. Clean off any residue on the threads with a toothbrush.

Installing a New Showerhead

Apply the Teflon tape to the exterior threads of the arm, wrapping it counterclockwise until you have 3 or 4 layers. Before installing the new showerhead, make sure that the washer is located inside it. Put the new showerhead on the end of the shower arm, turning it clockwise with your hand. Place the slip-joint pliers on the middle of the arm and secure. Put the rubber grip on the collar nut and position the adjustable wrench on it. Turn the nut clockwise to tighten.

Applying Teflon tape to threads of shower arm

Securing new showerhead

Turn *on* the shower and watch for leaks at the collar nut. If there aren't any, *bravo!* If there are, don't fret. Just try tightening the collar nut again.

If you need to replace a showerhead along with a shower arm, you might as well not separate them. Just leave the shower assembly in one piece, remove, and take to a plumbing supply or hardware store for replacement.

Removing old shower arm

REPLACING A SHOWER ARM

Removing an Old Shower Arm

Place both hands on the shower arm and turn it counterclockwise. If this doesn't loosen it from the wall, apply a lubricating spray to the base of the arm (where it connects to the wall). Try twisting it again, or use an adjustable wrench.

Installing a New Shower Arm

Before starting, wrap the head of the adjustable wrench with masking tape to prevent any marring of the new pipe. Next, apply 3 or 4 layers of Teflon tape counterclockwise around the exterior threads on both ends of the arm. Insert the arm into the connection in the wall and twist clockwise. Use the adjustable wrench to tighten the shower arm.

Insert the new showerhead onto the arm, twisting it clockwise. Use the adjustable wrench to tighten the head at the collar nut.

Turn *on* the shower and look for leaks at the 2 connections. If there are leaks, retighten the arm or head with the wrench.

Applying Teflon tape to threads of shower arm

Installing new shower arm

The majority of
cities throughout
the country require
a handheld shower
unit to be installed
with a vacuum
breaker, which
keeps the backflow
of water out of
the community's
water system, but
not all units come
with one. Check to
see if the new unit
comes with a
vacuum breaker, or
where you can
purchase one.

Installing a Handheld Shower Unit

Dottie's mother, Evangelia, was visiting for an extended period of time, so she decided to install a handheld shower unit in the guest bathroom. Dottie knew that it would make showering easier for her mom, but what she didn't know was how much nicer it would make her life, too. Once her kids started using the new showerhead, they fought over who would be first to take a shower. Who knows, showers today, tooth brushing tomorrow?

There are a lot of styles of handheld shower units, all with different instructions. Therefore, it's important to refer to the owner's manual throughout this installation. For

TOOLS NEEDED

- Towel • Masking tape • Slip-joint pliers or plumber's wrench
- Adjustable wrench • Lubricating spray • Rubber grip or wash cloth
- Teflon tape • New handheld shower unit
- Old toothbrush or wire brush

example, some models come with washers (a.k.a. gaskets) and others are washerless.

The following instructions explain how to install a handheld shower unit with a washer and a vacuum breaker.

Slip-joint pliers and adjustable wrench on shower arm

REMOVING THE OLD SHOWER HEAD

Wrap masking tape around the heads of the slip-joint pliers and adjustable wrench to protect the shower arm from being marred. Attach the slip-joint pliers to the top of the shower arm to keep it from rotating while you're trying to remove the head.

Applying Teflon tape to threads of shower arm

> **Place a towel over the bathtub drain to keep any small parts from falling down the drain.**

Position the rubber grip or washcloth on the collar nut and place the adjustable wrench on top of it, turning it counterclockwise to loosen. If the nut is difficult to unscrew, apply lubricating spray to it. Once the nut is loosened, you can continue unscrewing it by hand. Use a toothbrush to clean off any residue found on the threads.

Apply the Teflon tape to the exterior threads of the arm, wrapping it counterclockwise until you have three or four layers. Be sure to stretch the tape to get it into the grooves.

INSTALLING A HANDHELD SHOWER UNIT

Insert the vacuum breaker into the nut at the end of the hose, which attaches to the shower arm (if you install the vacuum breaker into the end of the hose that attaches to the *hand shower*, it will not work properly). Place the washer (if provided) firmly into the nut of the hose.

Place the hose on the end of the shower arm, turning it clockwise by hand until it's tightened. Insert the hand shower into the shower arm mount, rotating it to the desired position. Turn the shower *on* and look for leaks at

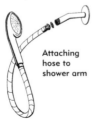

Attaching hose to shower arm

the connection. It's common for a hand shower with a vacuum breaker to drain for 1 or 2 seconds after the shower has been turned *off*. If there is a leak at the connection, use the adjustable wrench to tighten the nut.

SEASONAL REPAIRS

Winterizing Plumbing

As physicians, Alice and her husband fixed
ailing people. But if something needed fixing
around their house, they'd call a contractor
and flip a coin to see who'd have to stay home.
Alice realized they were spending too many of
their precious vacation days with the repairperson
instead of with each other. So, before the harsh
winter arrived, she decided to do some preventive
maintenance by first draining the water from her
home's exterior faucets and hoses. Now, instead
of thawing frozen pipes this cold winter, she
and her husband will be defrosting on a warm,
sunny beach.

You may not be ready to pull out your winter clothing,
but don't put off covering those exposed water pipes in
your home and winterizing your exterior water faucets.

TOOLS NEEDED

- Lubricating spray • Adjustable wrench
- Rag • Cold weather faucet cover

Exterior and interior shut-off valves

Opening bleeder cap on main water supply valve

PREPARING EXTERIOR FAUCETS

Whether you live in a new home with a frost-free exterior faucet or in an older home with a good ol' hose bib (common exterior faucet), your faucets are vulnerable during a harsh winter. The most important thing you can do to prevent faucets and pipes from freezing is to rid them of any water *before* winter.

First, you'll need to know if your home has an interior shut-off valve for the exterior faucet. Typically, the valve is located on the interior wall of the house, directly behind the exterior faucet, and will have either a gate valve (wheel-shaped) or a ball valve (lever). To shut it *off*, turn the gate valve clockwise or move the ball valve a quarter turn. If the gate valve is difficult to move, apply lubricating spray and use the adjustable wrench.

Go outside to the exterior faucet. Detach the garden hose, if applicable. Open the exterior faucet by turning the handle counterclockwise, allowing any water remaining in the pipe to drain.

Go back inside and open the bleeder cap ($3/8$-inch round brass cap) located on the side of the main water supply valve. Using the adjustable wrench, slightly turn the bleeder cap counterclockwise. Leave it open for several seconds to allow air into the pipes to help force any trapped water out. Use a rag to catch drops of water that may drain from the bleeder. Close the cap immediately.

After the water has drained from the exterior faucet, shut it *off*, turning it clockwise, to prevent cold air from entering the water pipes. For added protection, place the cold weather cover over the faucet and secure the hook (inside the cover)

Even if you have a frost-free exterior faucet, you still need to properly maintain it for the cold weather, because it's not 100 percent foolproof.

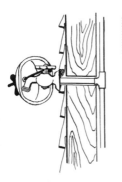

**Installing
cold weather
faucet cover**

around it. Turn the wing nut, located on the top of the cover, until it's tight.

Drain any water that may still be inside the garden hose by hanging it over your deck or fence. If you have neither, extend the hose its entire length. Raise one end to waist level and putting one hand in front of the other, walk the length of the hose, draining it of any trapped water. You may have to repeat this exercise a few times.

If you don't have an interior shut-off valve, have one installed by a licensed plumber.

INSULATING INTERIOR WATER PIPES

Installing insulation on exposed interior pipes, typically found in an unfinished basement, helps to prevent the

TOOLS NEEDED

• Interior pipe insulation (tube) • Utility knife
• Duct tape

pipes from freezing. There's no need to remove the insulation after winter, because it also aids in reducing the energy used by the water heater to warm the cold water, as well as in muffling the sounds of noisy pipes.

Interior pipe insulation comes in different materials, lengths, and circumferences, so don't go to the hardware store without knowing the size of your pipes. The standard size of residential pipes is $\frac{1}{2}$ inch and $\frac{3}{4}$ inch. If you don't know the size of the pipes, use a tape measure to find the correct circumference.

Installing Insulation

The insulation tube is pre-cut down the center so that you can easily place it around the pipe. Peel off the tape found on both edges and stick the two together, working your way down the length of the tube. If you will be using more than one insulation tube, you may need to cut the tubing to size with the utility knife. Cut the duct tape and wrap the pieces where the tubes meet.

Taping pre-cut insulation

Thawing a Frozen Water Pipe

Some women go to Jamaica to get their groove back—Yvonne was going there to get one. While she was chillin' in the sun, her home's water pipes were chillin' in a record cold spell. The pipes burst, spewing tons of water into her home. The water rose above the furnace and went out into the street, where it iced over, forcing the city to close the road. Yvonne returned to a condemned house, angry neighbors, and a water bill equal to her Jamaican trip.

The best preventive measures in freezing weather are to leave a faucet dripping at a slow rate, open the cabinets to allow the warm air in the room to reach the pipes exposed to the exterior wall, and wrap the exposed interior water pipes with insulation (see "Winterizing Plumbing," page 89).

Water in a pipe can freeze when two things occur simultaneously: 1) the outside temperature goes below freezing; and 2) an exterior or interior water pipe is not properly insulated.

There will be no mistaking when a water pipe has burst in your home, but how can you tell when a pipe is freezing or has frozen? A pipe that is freezing

TOOLS NEEDED

- Flashlight • Hair dryer
- Extension cord

emits *extremely* cold water. If a pipe is frozen, then *no* water will come out of the faucet.

IF A PIPE HAS BURST

An emergency fix for a burst water pipe is to immediately shut *off* the main water supply valve (see "The Main Water Supply Valve: How to Find It and Shut It Off," page 6). If there is standing water, do *not* turn on any electrical switches—use a flashlight instead. Contact a certified plumber . . . and your insurance agent!

Heating frozen pipe with hair dryer

IF A PIPE IS FROZEN

Use a hair dryer (with an extension cord, if necessary) to heat a frozen pipe. Because it's almost impossible to see where the freeze originated, you'll have to heat the entire length of the pipe. This could take as long as 20 to 30 minutes. Turn the faucet *on* and wait about 3 minutes. If water is still not coming out, try reheating the pipe.

Clearing a Gutter and Downspout

> The first home repair Olivia ever did was out of
> necessity, because as a single parent raising
> four children on limited funds, a leaky roof didn't
> fit into her budget. She asked her neighbors for help,
> but none of the women had ever been on a ladder,
> let alone a roof. As Olivia was climbing up,
> her neighbors were yelling for her to stop her
> nonsense and get down. But when she held up
> the cause of the leak—an overthrown newspaper
> which clogged the gutter—they shouted, "You go,
> girl!" Olivia's 15 minutes of fame came and
> went (as well as the leak), but her gutters are
> still going strong.

Gutters and downspouts are the main parts of the
exterior drainage system of your house. This system
can carry thousands of gallons of water every year, so
it's important to properly maintain it—once in the
spring and again in the fall. Don't be fooled into think-
ing a heavy rain will clean the gutters for you, because
it can actually make things worse. Decayed leaves
and mud can block the flow of water in the gutters
and downspouts and corrode them with mineral
deposits.

Cleaning the gutter system is not a difficult job; however, it can be time consuming, depending on the number of gutters and downspouts you have and on the amount of accumulated debris. If the gutter is clogged, you'll have to clean it in sections, which means moving the ladder and climbing up and down it several times.

For safety reasons, don't tackle this job if the ground is wet or, if it's very windy outside, be sure to wear shoes with good traction, and follow the rules for ladder safety (see "Practicing Ladder Safety," page 120).

We recommend you hire a contractor to do repairs such as fixing rust spots, holes, and leaking seams, tightening the fasteners that secure the gutter system to the house, and adjusting the slope of the gutter.

Removing leaf guard

CLEARING A GUTTER

Decide which section of the house you're going to tackle first. With your friend's help, place the ladder at the end of the gutter farthest from the downspout. Using a tape measure, check that the ladder is correctly angled against the exterior wall (see "Practicing Ladder Safety," page 120).

Climb the ladder, carrying the garden hose, bucket, and trowel. Go high enough so that you can see into the gutter and hook the nozzle of the hose to the rung above you. If your gutter has a leaf guard,

TOOLS NEEDED

- Shoes with good traction
- Helpful friend • Ladder
- Tape measure
- Garden hose with spray nozzle
- Bucket or a plastic grocery bag
- Garden trowel or scoop

flip it up, or remove and place on the roof above where it was located.

If you find a small amount of debris in the gutter, spray it toward the downspout. If the gutter is clear, secure the leaf guard into place.

For a large amount of debris, remove it with the trowel and place the debris in the bucket. Climb down the ladder and empty the debris-filled bucket into a trash can. With your friend's help, move the ladder to the next section of gutter to be cleaned. Work your way down the entire length of the gutter until it is completely cleared of debris. Secure the leaf guard into place.

Placing gutter debris into bucket

Spraying debris toward downspout

With your friend's help again, move the ladder back to the end of the gutter farthest from the downspout (the same spot where you started). Climb the ladder with the garden hose and spray any remaining debris toward the downspout. If there is standing water in the gutter, then the downspout may be clogged or the gutter is not properly sloped.

Repeat this procedure for all of your home's gutters.

Flushing debris through downspout

CLEARING A DOWNSPOUT

With your friend's help, move the ladder close to the downspout. Climb the ladder, carrying the garden hose, going high enough so that you can feed it into the downspout.

Have your friend turn on the water, and wash the debris

TOOLS NEEDED

• Shoes with good traction
• Helpful friend • Extension ladder
• Garden hose (without spray nozzle)

down the spout. If there is still standing water in the gutter, then the gutter may not be sloped enough to allow for proper drainage. We recommend you hire a contractor to adjust the gutter's slope.

Walk around to every downspout and make sure that each one has a splash block and that it's positioned correctly so that water is directed away from the house, not toward it.

Downspout with splash block

Remember to wear shoes with good traction and follow the rules for ladder safety.

Bleeding a Hot Water Radiator

> If your radiator is whistlin' while it's workin',
> that's not because it's happy. Whistling is a
> sign that it needs maintenance.

A water system heats the home by bringing hot water
from the boiler through the pipes and into the radiators
or convectors. You can see by the illustrations that radiators and convectors differ in appearance, even though
they provide the same service.

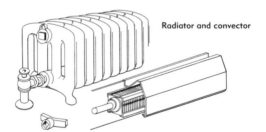

Radiator and convector

TOOLS NEEDED

- Rag • Vacuum with brush attachment • Needlenose pliers
- Cup • Valve key or flathead screwdriver

To help this heating system run efficiently, you need to clean it regularly and bleed it every fall. To bleed a radiator means to remove the hot air trapped inside that is blocking the flow of heat. Older radiators typically require a valve key to turn the bleeder valve; if not, a screwdriver may work.

If your hot water system uses convectors, check for any bent fins and straighten them with needlenose pliers. Some convectors have the same bleed valves as radiators; if yours doesn't, contact a certified plumber to have the system professionally maintained.

Use the rag and vacuum with brush attachment to clean all of the radiators before bleeding them.

Always keep furniture away from a radiator and never paint it, as paint will block the flow of air.

Bleeding radiator

Turn the thermostat up high enough so that the furnace turns *on*. If you live in a multi-storied house, start with the radiator on the highest level; if you don't, start with the one farthest from the boiler. With one hand holding the cup underneath the bleeder valve, insert the valve key or screwdriver into the valve and turn it counterclockwise to open.

Once the hissing sound of escaping air stops, water will begin to dribble out. Quickly turn the valve *off*, being careful to avoid the hot steam and water that may spew out. Repeat this process on all of the radiators or convectors.

During the winter months when the heat is on in your

home, periodically check the radiators to see if any are cold to the touch. Bleed any that are, starting with the one farthest from the boiler. If a radiator still is not producing heat, contact a certified plumber.

If you live in an apartment, remember that landlords are required by law to provide heat—not air conditioning, though. If the heat in your apartment isn't working, first notify your landlord. If this doesn't bring about a change, contact your city government.

APPLIANCES

Freeing a Jammed Garbage Disposal

A garbage disposal is not a necessity . . . until it's broken. We asked some women what the craziest things were that jammed their garbage disposals, and here's what they said: a baby food jar, a set of keys, and our personal favorite—a dozen red roses that our friend Pam decapitated one at a time (it was a liberating experience, she said).

If you hear an unusual humming or buzzing noise when you turn on the garbage disposal, it's jammed. Resist the urge to grind the object into oblivion—no matter how bad your day was! The garbage disposal's over-load protector automatically

Never put chicken skin, grease, plastic, glass, meat bones, fruit peel and pits, or a drain cleaner into the garbage disposal.

TOOLS NEEDED

- Flashlight
- Needlenose pliers or tongs
- ¼-inch Allen wrench or broom-stick handle

shuts off the motor to protect it from burning out. This safety feature also serves to protect the electrical wiring within your home. Some disposals reset themselves automatically after 15 to 30 minutes. Other models have a reset button which, when pushed, resets it. This is found on the exterior base of the disposal motor.

Turning flywheel with Allen wrench

Some garbage disposals have a reversal feature, which allows the flywheel (the rotating plate that shreds the waste) inside the disposal to operate in reverse to free the obstruction. The reversal feature is automatically activated each time the unit is switched on. Other garbage disposals have a hole in the exterior base of the unit where a $1/4$-inch Allen wrench can be inserted to turn the flywheel (some units come with the wrench). If in doubt, check the appliance owner's manual or contact the manufacturer.

FIRST TRY THIS

Turn the electrical on/off switch that operates the garbage disposal to the *off* position. Use the flashlight to look inside the disposal for the lodged object. Remove it using tongs or pliers.

IF THAT DOESN'T WORK

If you can't locate the object *and* your disposal has a reversal feature, run the cold-water faucet and turn *on* the disposal. It may be necessary to turn the disposal *on* and *off* several times to activate the reversal feature.

IF YOUR DISPOSAL DOES *NOT* HAVE A REVERSAL FEATURE

Turn *off* the main power by removing a fuse or flipping the circuit breaker. Locate the hole on the bottom of the disposal under the sink and insert the Allen wrench into the hole. Work the wrench in both directions, counterclockwise and clockwise until it turns fully in complete circles.

If you don't have an Allen wrench, stick the broomstick handle into the disposal, resting it against the blades. Using the same technique as with the wrench,

turn the handle counterclockwise and clockwise to dislodge
the obstruction.

After freeing the jam, remove
the dislodged material with
tongs and restore the power.
Push the reset button (which
activates the overload protector) and run cold water for
about 1 minute. Turn *on* the
garbage disposal. If the disposal still won't start, wait 15
minutes for the motor to cool
fully and press the reset button
again.

If the object just won't budge,
then contact the manufacturer
for a list of professional repair
persons in your area.

Allen wrench inserted
into the bottom hole of
garbage disposal

Finger depressing
reset button on
garbage disposal

Repairing a Slow-Filling Washing Machine

The Novellas is a women's book club bound
together by years of meetings and shared lives.
But after fifteen years, the members decided they
needed to add a new chapter to their lives by
becoming a home repair club. Each month a member
chose a repair that needed to be done in her home
and everyone arrived ready for the challenge. The
first repair was fixing a slow-filling washing machine.
It didn't take long for those female bookworms to
be repair-literate, too, and the repairs were so easy
no one needed Cliff Notes!

If your washing machine is taking a long time to fill up
with water, the likely culprits are the inlet screens.
These are located inside the inlet valve holes, which are
found on the back of the washing machine where the
hot and cold hoses connect to it. These small screens
protect the hoses from becoming clogged with debris. If
particles are trapped inside the hoses, water is not able
to flow freely into the washing machine.

TOOLS NEEDED

- Masking tape • Pencil • Old toothbrush
- Slip-joint pliers • Bucket • Small bowl
- Metal fingernail file or flathead screwdriver • White vinegar

If you can't find screens in your washing machine inlet valves, there could be two reasons: 1) in areas where hard water is prevalent, inlet filters are deliberately not installed because the sediment in hard water can clog a screen very quickly and most people won't go to the trouble of cleaning them; or 2) the screen is strategically placed in a hard-to-get-to

Turning off
water supply valve

spot so that people won't remove it. When in doubt, refer to the owner's manual or contact the manufacturer.

Unplug the washing machine, or turn *off* the power at the main service panel, and pull it out as far as possible so you can get behind it. Turn *off* the water supply valve(s) located on the wall behind the washing machine.

You'll see that the washing machine has two inlet hoses—one for hot water and one for cold (hot is typically located on the left; cold on the right). Each hose is attached to the appliance at the inlet valves, and each valve contains a small inlet screen.

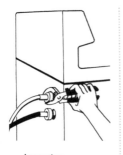

**Loosening
coupling nuts**

Before removing the hoses, tear off two pieces of masking tape and mark one "hot" and the other "cold," and tape them to their respective hoses. Use the slip-joint pliers to loosen the coupling nuts by turning them counterclockwise. Remove the hoses and pour the water into the utility sink or bucket.

Locate the inlet screens in the valves and pop them out with a metal fingernail file, being careful not to tear the screens. You can choose to clean the inlet screens or replace them with new ones. To clean the screens, soak them in white vinegar for 15 minutes, gently scrub with the toothbrush, and rinse with warm water. Return the old or new inlet screen to each valve.

Reconnect the hoses to the washing machine, noting the labels on the tape. Tighten the coupling nuts by turning them clockwise, making certain not to over-tighten. Restore power to the appliance, turn *on* the water, and push the washing machine back into place.

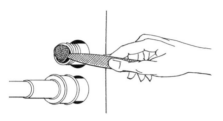

Removing inlet screens

Setting a Water Heater's Temperature

For the past 22 of her 78 years, Laurel has been a widow living alone on a fixed income. She was blessed with neighbors who were always willing to fix things around her house, but she began to feel that it was time to dare to tackle some of the projects herself. Laurel decided to start small by changing the temperature of her water heater. With a few successes under her tool belt, she began visiting her widowed friends to show them how to do small home repairs. "Who says you can't teach an old dog new tricks!" boasts Laurel.

Do you know how hot your water temperature is? Water temperature that is 140°F can produce first-degree burns within 3 seconds. You can ensure your water will be at a safe temperature by adjusting the setting of the water heater to 120°F. If you live in an apartment, have your superintendent install an anti-scalding device on your faucets. (Most new water heaters are preset to 120°F before shipment by the manufacturer.)

TOOLS NEEDED
• Candy thermometer • Watch

TESTING THE WATER'S TEMPERATURE

Before you make any adjustments to your water heater, first take your water's temperature.

Run the hot water in your bathtub or sink for approximately 5 minutes. With the hot water still running, hold the thermometer underneath for about 1 minute. Turn *off* the water and read the temperature on the thermometer. If the temperature reads above 120°F, you'll need to change the setting of the hot water heater. After you've adjusted the setting, wait 1 hour before retesting the water temperature.

Thermometer under running water

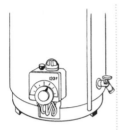

Temperature dial on water heater

CHANGING THE SETTING OF A GAS WATER HEATER

A gas water heater has a temperature control knob located near the bottom that is used to adjust water temperature. Some knobs have words such as "vacation," "energy saving," "warm," "hot," or "hotter," or they have markings or indentations with temperature readings of 120°F, 130°F, 140°F, and 150°F. Some knobs will have both words and markings.

Before beginning, read the instructions located on the large label on the water heater or in the owner's manual.

TOOL NEEDED

• Owner's manual

Locate the thermostat control knob near the bottom of the water heater. If the knob clearly states 120°F, then turn it to that marking. If you are unsure as to which word denotes 120°F, check the owner's manual or contact the manufacturer.

Running the faucet for 5 minutes wastes a lot of water, so perform this test after taking a shower, when the water is already hot!

CHANGING THE SETTING OF AN ELECTRIC WATER HEATER

An electric water heater has either one or two panel doors on the front with the thermostats behind them. The thermostat control knob allows you to adjust the temperature of the water heater and contains markings or indentations with temperature readings of

Moving aside insulation

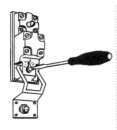

Adjusting thermostat

120°F, 130°F, 140°F, and 150°F. Some models require you to adjust one thermostat and others require you to adjust both. If you're unsure, check the owner's manual or contact the manufacturer.

Before beginning, read the instructions located on the large label on the water heater or in the owner's manual.

Turn *off* the power to the water heater at the main service panel. Remove the panel door(s) and move the insulation away from the thermostat. Do not remove the plastic cover.

TOOLS NEEDED

- Owner's manual
- Flathead screwdriver

Use the screwdriver to adjust the thermostat to 120°F. Depress the reset button (typically red). Replace the insulation, making sure that the thermostat is well covered, and replace the panel door(s). Restore the power to the water heater.

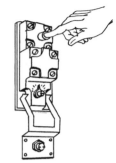

Depressing reset button

PRACTICING
LADDER SAFETY

At 5 feet 10 inches, Donna was a walking stepladder, but even she couldn't reach everything in her home. Never wanting to take the time to look for the stepladder, Donna would instead find creative substitutes: a bureau, kitchen countertop, and all types of chairs. It wasn't until she had a bad fall that she was brought down to size.

Once you've chosen the right ladder for the job, adhere to the following rules:

- Don't place a ladder near overhead electrical wires.
- Don't go up a ladder if the ground is wet or it's a windy day.
- Never climb higher than the third rung from the top.
- Always keep your hips between the side rails with your legs spread slightly for balance.
- Never have more than one person on the ladder.
- Carry the ladder parallel to the ground.
- Check to be sure that the ladder is level before climbing.

- **Never overreach.**
- **Hold on to the ladder with at least one hand.**

To determine the correct angle at which to place the ladder against the exterior wall, use this formula: Length of ladder/4 = Correct Angle. For example, if the length of the ladder you are using is 16 feet, then the equation will be 16 feet/4 = 4 feet. Therefore, the distance between the ladder and the wall should be 4 feet.

There are four types of ladders most commonly used around the home:

1. **stepladder**
2. **straight ladder**
3. **extension ladder**
4. **sectional ladder**

A stepladder, the shortest of the ladders, has two or three steps and a spreader on each side that locks into place. A straight ladder comes in heights ranging from 4 to 12 feet. An extension ladder is typically 16 feet long but can extend to 40 feet. A sectional ladder transforms into an A-frame or extension ladder.

INDEX

"DARE TO REPAIR" BOOKS
by Julie Sussman and Stephanie Glakas-Tenet

DARE TO REPAIR
A Do-It-Yourself Guide to Fixing
(Almost) Anything in the Home
ISBN 0-06-095984-3

Provides even the most repair-challenged woman
with the ability to successfully fix things around the
home. Once you start, you won't want to stop.

DARE TO REPAIR YOUR CAR
A Do-It-Yourself Guide to Maintenance,
Safety, Minor Fix-Its, and Talking Shop
ISBN 0-06-057700-2

Removes the road blocks to learning basic car care by
offering women simple instructions on maintenance,
safety, minor repairs, and how to talk to mechanics.

Visit www.AuthorTracker.com
for exclusive updates on your favorite authors.

Available wherever books are sold,
or call 1-800-331-3761 to order.